Can't stand working with these people

Secretly looking for another job

Upset
about
your
promotion

Don't enjoy dealing with coworkers

Don't agree with company policies

Only here
because
can't
find
anything
better

Don't
get
along
with
coworkers

Can't stand the way you talk to me

Don't think you're qualified

Only pretending to be interested in meeting

Want
to quit
and
never
return

I'll try
being
nicer if
you'll try
being
smarter

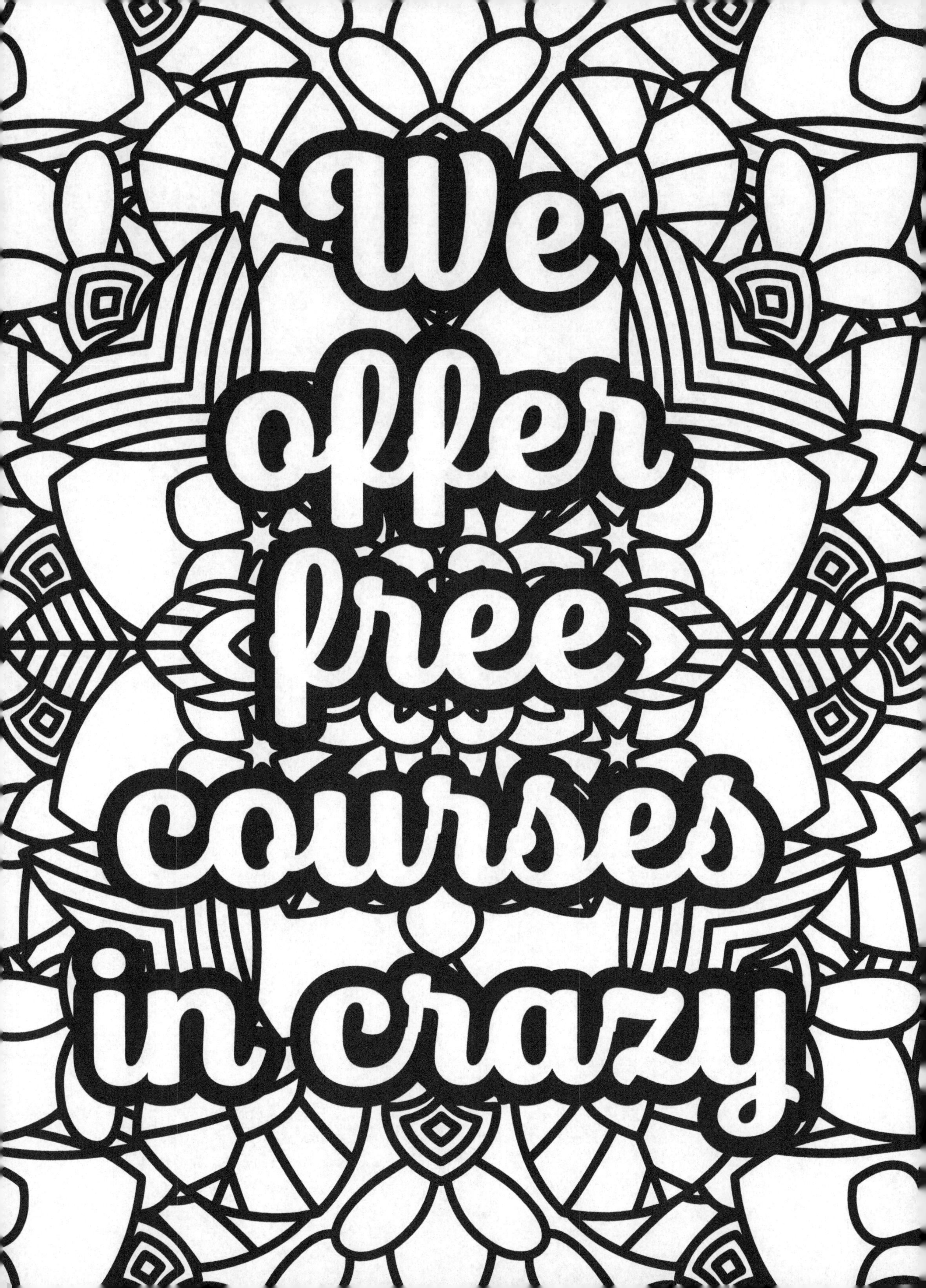
We
offer
free
courses
in crazy

I don't
get
paid
enough
for this

Is never
f*cking
good
for
you?

I gave
zero
f*cks
today

No,
I can't
work this
weekend
motherf*cker

F*ck You

That
question
is not
topic
related
f*cker

All this
time, and
you
haven't
done
sh*t

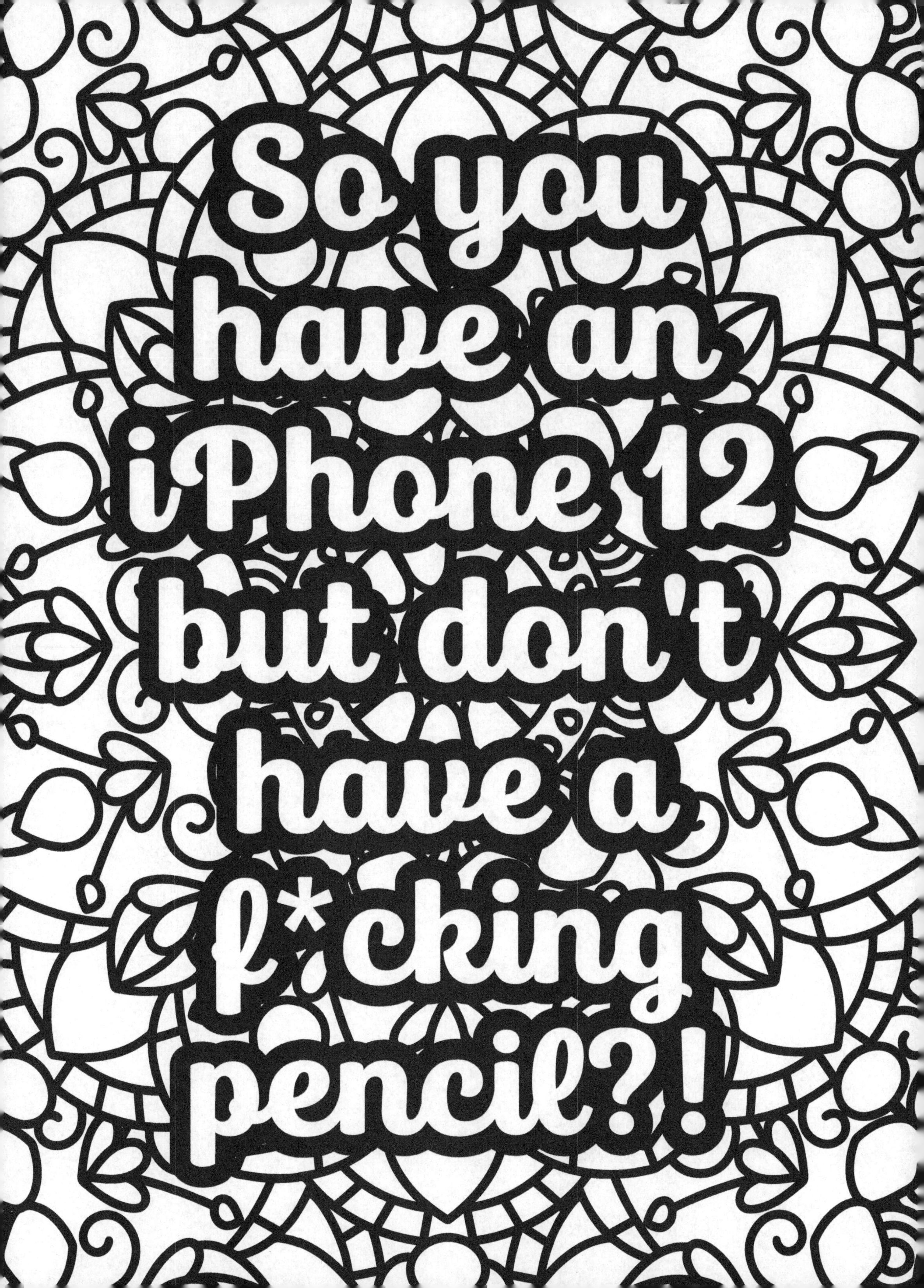
So you have an iPhone 12 but don't have a f*cking pencil?!

Sit
your
as*
down

Screw this! I'm going home

Friday
is my
second
favorite
f-word

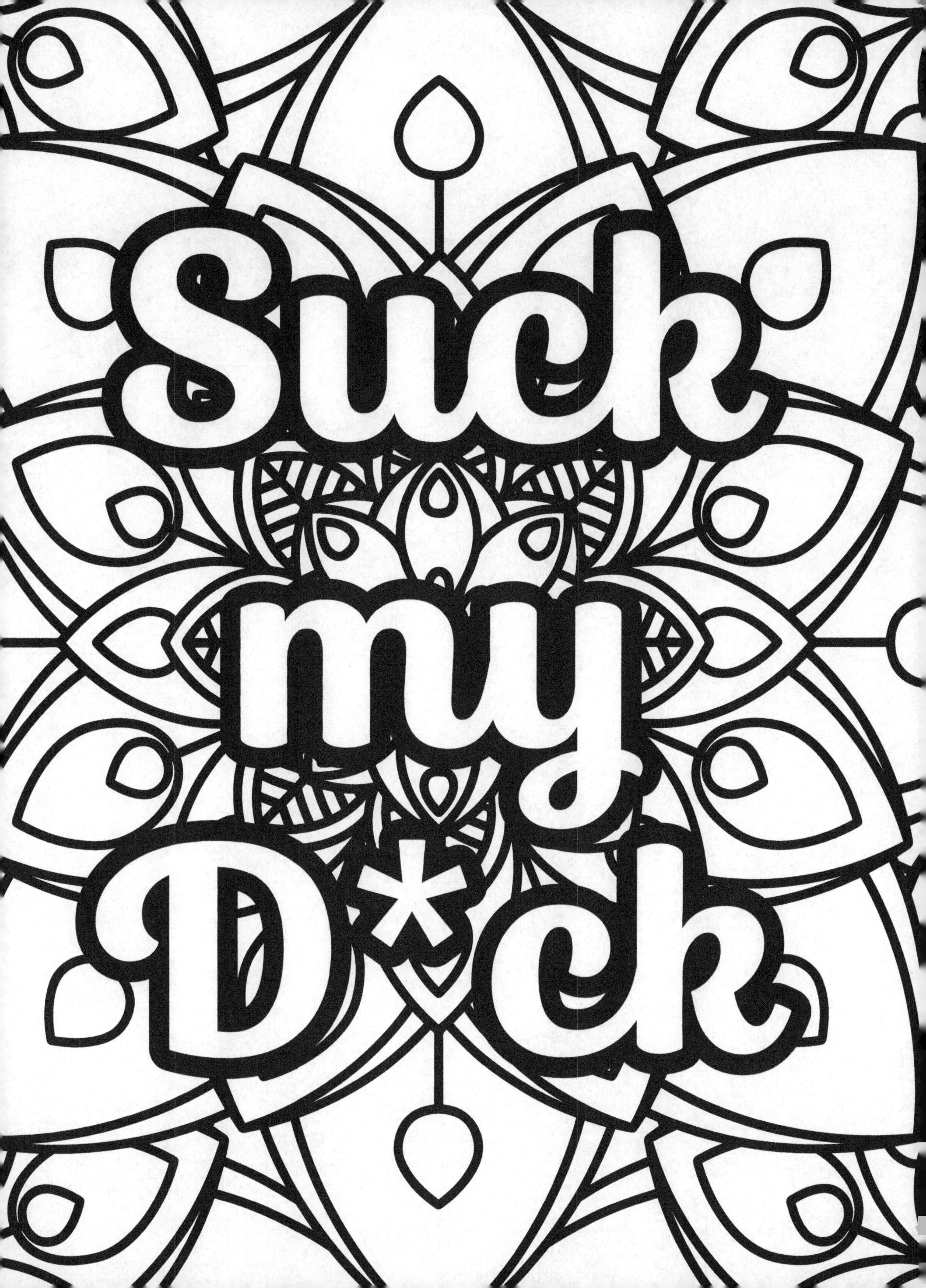
Suck
my
D*ck

Who the f*ck moved my stapler?

Why is the printer jammed?

Need
a
vacation,
starting
now

Why is the coffee always gone?

Not a
f*cking
Monday
person

Another sh*t day here

I run on
caffeine,
chaos,
and
curse
words

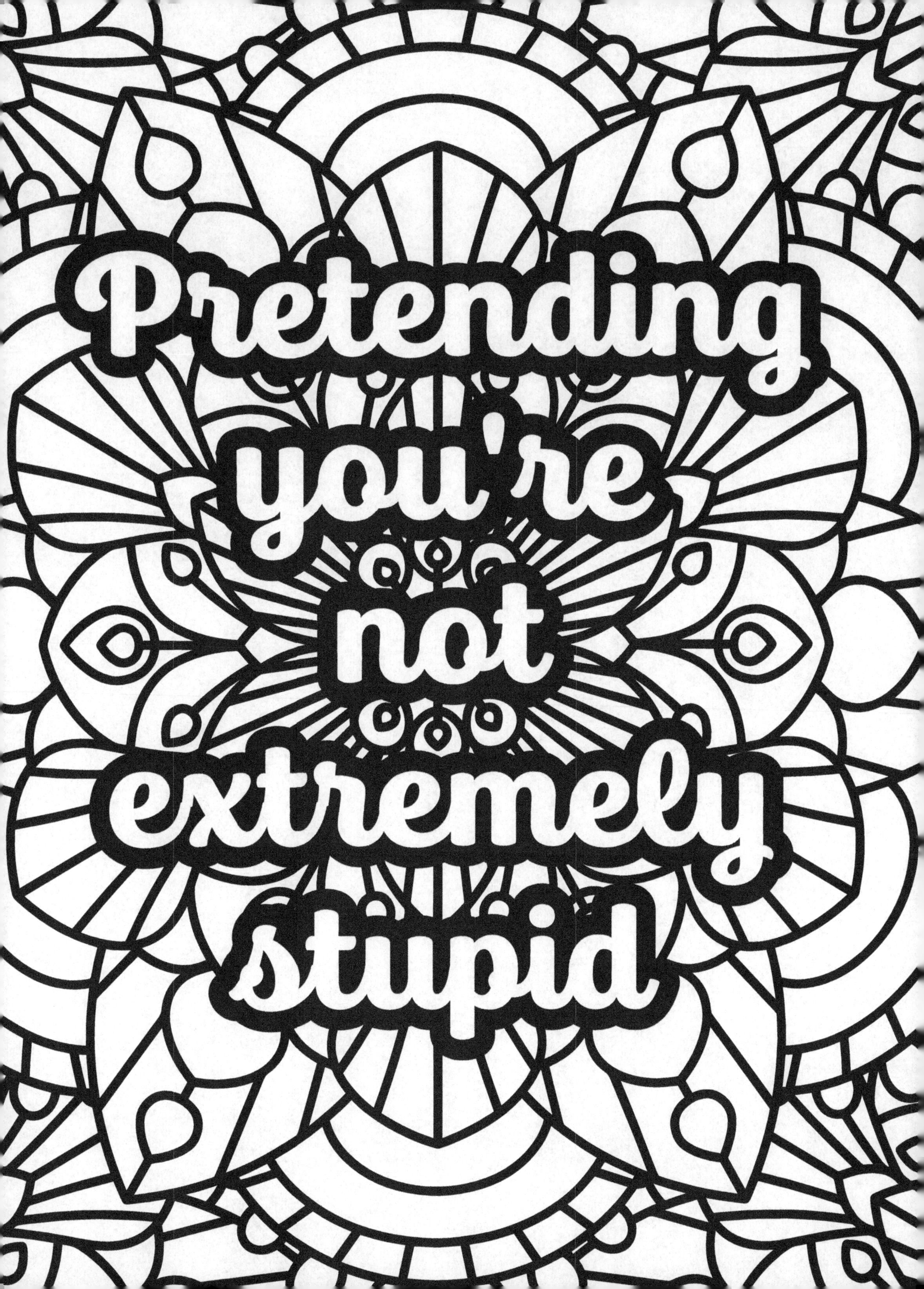
Pretending
you're
not
extremely
stupid

Is this
a
special
ed
class?!?

F*cking
chaos
coordinator

I'm seriously out of f*cks today

Sh*t! Work is back

I suffer
from
resting
work
face

The
instant
worker
just
add
coffee

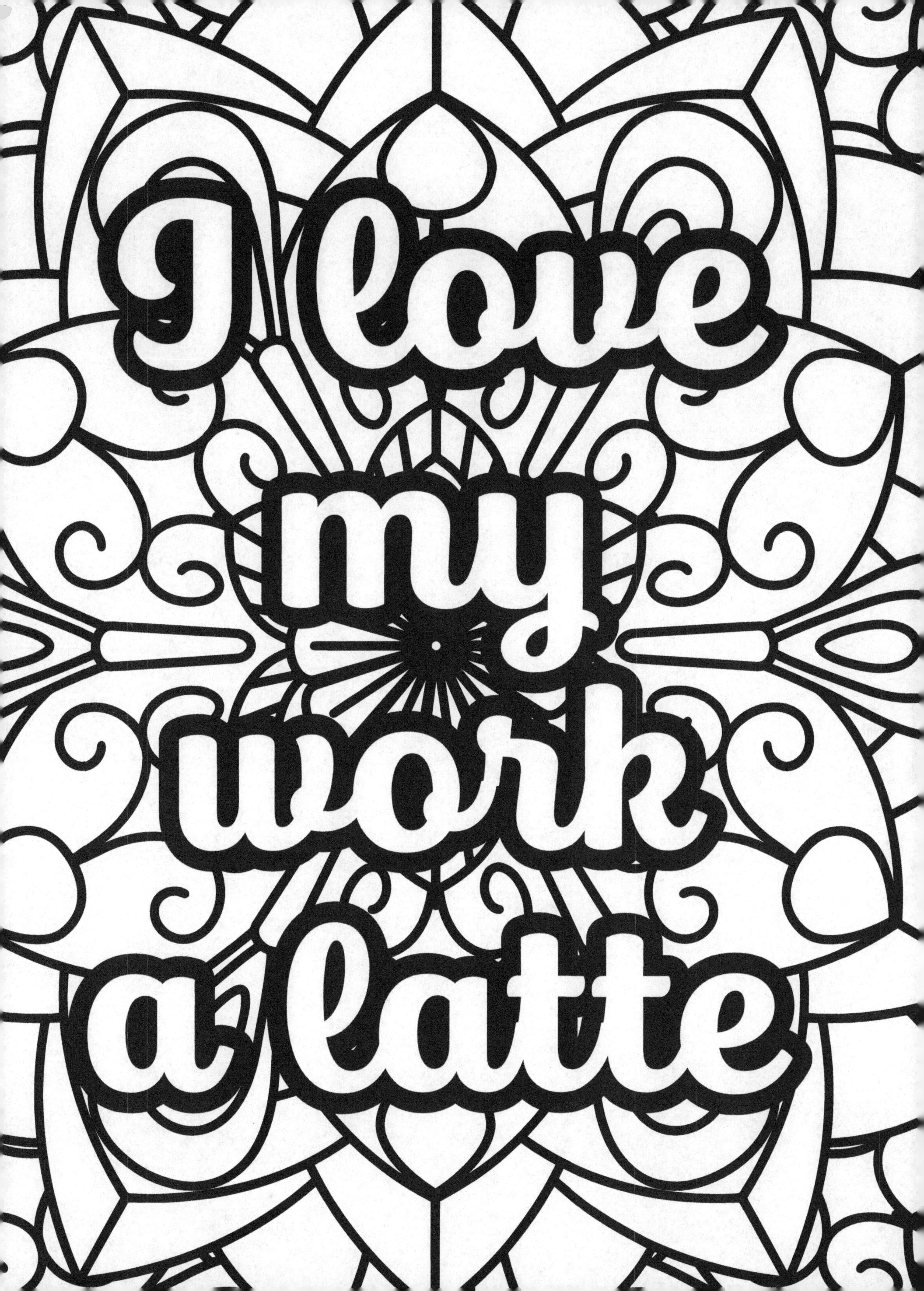
I love
my
work
a latte

Worker?
I prefer
f*cking
rockstar

I'm not
your
f*cking
babysitter

I
need a
mother
-f*cking
drink

STFU
Just
assume
I'm
always
right

I wish
some
workers
were
fluent
in silence

May choke in all the sh*t you talk

Death
before
decaf

You inspire my inner serial killer

I wish
I could
invoice
you for
wasting
my time

I need
a hug..e
bottle
of
wine

Made in the USA
Las Vegas, NV
03 November 2023

80188048R00057